Original title:
Into the Ivy

Copyright © 2025 Creative Arts Management OÜ
All rights reserved.

Author: Cassandra Whitaker
ISBN HARDBACK: 978-1-80567-250-0
ISBN PAPERBACK: 978-1-80567-549-5

Where Nature Weaves its Tales

In the garden, squirrels play,
Chasing shadows, day by day.
One lost its nut, a funny plight,
It scolded trees all through the night.

A cat on branches, looking proud,
Tried to impress a passing crowd.
But slipped and tumbled, what a sight,
Landed soft, in flowers bright.

A Symphony of Leaves

Leaves are dancing in a breeze,
Tickling plants and teasing bees.
A crow caws with a hint of sass,
While ants march on, a little class.

The wind plays tunes on wooden bows,
As nature whispers, 'Shhh, it knows!'
A branch bows low, it feels so fine,
And squirrels sigh, 'We'll drink some wine!'

The Canvas of Climbing Whispers

Vines twist up, a ladder high,
Reaching out to flirt and pry.
A raccoon grins, his paws in mud,
Dreaming of a tasty bud.

Flowers giggle as they bloom,
Reminding bees to clear the gloom.
They buzz about, in quite a fuss,
As petals dance, without a bus.

Dreaming Beneath the Overhead Tangle

In the shade, I lie and grin,
With twirling leaves, I feel the spin.
A butterfly lands on my nose,
Saying, 'Hey there, how it goes?'

Above, the branches chat in glee,
Telling tales they hold with glee.
A squirrel squeaks from high above,
'Hey, stop staring, show some love!'

Tangled in the Embrace of Green

I tried to walk, but oh dear me,
My shoelaces danced like leaves on a tree.
With roots that twist and twirl around,
I'm stuck in this charming, leafy playground.

My hat is caught on a branch up high,
As squirrels giggle and birds just fly.
A leafy hug, I can't escape,
A comical mess in nature's drape.

A Charmed Life Among the Tendrils

In a garden where the vines grow tall,
I tripped and stumbled, what a fall!
With petals tickling my silly nose,
I laughed so hard, I struck a pose.

A snake of ivy wrapped so tight,
I thought I'd have to spend the night.
But nature whispered, "Just have fun,"
So I danced beneath the shining sun.

The Hidden World Beneath the Leaves

Beneath the leaves, a world of cheer,
A toadstool party, come gather near.
With bugs in hats and ants that prance,
You'll find them all in a silly dance.

I peeked beneath where mysteries play,
A frog in a tux said, "Hip-hip-hooray!"
With every step, I felt alive,
In this wacky world, we will thrive.

Secrets Woven in Nature's Fabric

Oh, what secrets the garden hides,
A patchwork cloak where laughter abides.
A spider spins tales with a twist,
In a web of yarn, I can't resist.

The daisies chuckle, the daisies wink,
While I mumble words, I hardly think.
With petals ruffled and roots that tease,
I'm wrapped in joyous, leafy ease.

Dreams Woven in Green

Under the leaves where squirrels chatter,
I lost my hat, but found a platter.
A picnic spot with ants in tow,
They dance on crumbs, stealing the show.

A frog in shades declares it's cool,
While twigs like flags make nature's school.
We laugh and weave our dreams so bright,
In a leafy realm where every day's light.

The Mystery of Climbing Shadows

Beneath the boughs of mystery tall,
Mysterious shapes sneak, trip, and fall.
A cat creeps up, a leaf on her tail,
She thinks she's stealthy, but lands in a fail.

The shadows stretch, they seem to prance,
In this leafy realm, it's pure happenstance.
A jester breeze sweeps through with glee,
Tickling the trees like it's on a spree.

A Journey Through the Green Abyss

In a jungle gym of green galore,
I tumble and roll, what's behind that door?
A chipmunk laughs, he thinks I'm a clown,
As I trip on roots and tumble down.

The vines entwine, like old friends you meet,
They whisper secrets, a leafy retreat.
Jump over puddles, duck under twigs,
Life's a circus, come join the jigs!

The Song of Climbing Vines

A melody plays where the green things grow,
Vines serenade with a subtle show.
A parrot clown brings a colorful jest,
While plants gossip, they never rest.

From below, squirrels join the tune,
With drumming paws, they dance 'neath the moon.
In this verdant land of giggles and cheer,
Nature's a stage, so let's give a cheer!

Echoes of Nature's Embrace

In the woods where squirrels chat,
Laughter dances, where the wild things sat.
A tree branch wiggles with a glee,
While birds gossip, eyeing me.

A fox prances with a funny style,
Almost tripping, but with a smile.
The brook giggles, bubbling so bright,
As the sun plays tag with shadows light.

A Tangle of Dreams

In the garden, a gnome once dreamed,
Wishing for flowers that giggle and beamed.
A daisy tickles a bumblebee's wing,
As a worm whispers, 'Oh, what fun it'll bring!'

The butterflies dance in a chaotic spree,
Trying to land, look at them flee!
With petals swirling as they glide,
Nature's humor, they can't hide.

Secrets in the Leafy Labyrinth

In the maze of greens, a rabbit grins,
With carrots hidden, let the hunt begin.
A raccoon stumbles on a berry feast,\nWhile the owl
chuckles, 'You're quite the beast!'

Leaves rustle with mischievous whisper,
Telling tales of the morning crisper.
The shadows play tricks, hide and seek,
Nature's giggles make the wild unique.

Caress of the Climbing Shadows

As the sun sets, shadows stretch high,
A raccoon balances, oh my, oh my!
The tree limbs sway with a creaky laugh,
While fireflies plot their evening path.

A squirrel stashes acorns with flair,
In a hurry, he fumbles, what a rare scare!
The bushes rustle, catching a breeze,
Nature winks as it aims to please.

The Whispering Ivy's Tale

There once was a vine with a curious smile,
It tickled the rocks, made them laugh for a while.
With leaves all a-flutter, it wriggled with glee,
Whispering secrets to ants, one, two, three!

The sun gave a wink, the clouds puffed in fluff,
The vine told a joke; 'Can you handle this stuff?'
Every branch had a story, each tendril a jest,
A comedy show from nature, simply the best!

Birds perched in glee, with their beaks all agape,
They chirped in delight, "There's no room for escape!"
The ivy just chuckled, then twisted around,
Wrapping the laughter all up in the ground.

So if you should wander where green shadows play,
Listen for giggles hidden deep in the sway.
You'll find that the ivy is clever and spry,
With stories and laughter in each leafy sigh.

Beneath the Cloaking Green

Under leaves quite thick, where the sunlight won't peek,
Lies a party of critters, all dancing unique.
The snails brought the snacks, while the frogs sang a tune,

Beneath the thick canopy, hiding from noon.

The acorns were rolling, they spun with a grin,
While the ladybugs counted their spots, oh what din!
From the shadows emerged, a chipmunk with flair,
It juggled, it pranced, then tripped on fresh air.

A raccoon with shades made a trendy debut,
While the ivy just chuckled at all the hullabaloo.
"You're funnier than me!" bustled cobalt blue jay,
As they rallied together, then scampered away.

So should you find shrubs with a hue that is lush,
Join the verdant fiesta—no need to rush!
Laughs echo through green where the best jokes abound,
Underneath cloaking green, silliness found.

Vines of Memory

In gardens of yore, where the memories cling,
Each vine tells a story, it's quite the fun thing!
There's a grapevine that giggles, recalling the past,
With tales of grand picnics, how long will they last?

Its leafy nostalgia wraps 'round like a hug,
Remembering moments, the joyous and snug.
The daisies roll laughter from years gone by,
While the ivy, amused, whispers sweet lullabies.

But beware of the thorns, for they tend to complain,
"If you tug on our roots, we will surely disdain!"
Yet the blossoms just chuckle, and dance in the breeze,
For vines of sweet memory bring hearts to their knees.

So linger awhile where the green spirits roam,
The laughter of plants makes you feel right at home.
In this garden of giggles, let time drift away,
Among vines of sweet memory, come laugh and stay.

Tangled Stories of Forgotten Echoes

In a twist of the green, where the old echoes stay,
Lies a patch of confusion that loves to play!
Branches tie themselves in a silly old knot,
With tales of mishaps that amusingly plot.

The squirrel lost his acorns in a fit of grand glee,
While a hedgehog danced awkwardly under a tree.
Frogs croaked the chorus of a tune out of time,
As the ivy shook branches, now tangled in rhyme.

Grasshoppers hopped in, all wearing a grin,
"Let's tell a tall tale, or better, join in!"
Each leaf joined the chatter, while shadows would peek,
At the tangled up stories that tickled the cheek.

So next time you stroll where the greenery gleams,
Listen close to the echoes that float in daydreams.
For tangled stories bloom under playful guise,
A laughter-filled garden, oh such a surprise!

The Dance of the Forgotten Roots

Beneath the wiggle of the ground,
Old roots are jiving all around.
With twirls and dips in leafy caps,
They throw a party for the naps.

Worms groove close, their moves so slick,
They shimmy right with every tick.
The soil hums a silly tune,
As mushrooms burst to dance, too, soon.

Twirling tendrils up through the air,
Forget-me-nots join in with flair.
A wiggle here and shuffle there,
This root ballet is beyond compare.

When darkness falls, the critters cheer,
For nighttime brings the gophers near.
In shadowed bliss, they join the thing,
These hidden roots, they sure can swing!

Veils of Nature's Secrets

The leaves hang low with giggling tricks,
Whispering tales of nature's fix.
A spider spins a web of jest,
Trapping laughs, it's nature's best.

With every flitter, bugs will prance,
They take their time, no need to rush the dance.
A squirrel, too, with cheeky glee,
Practices his acorn jubilee.

The flowers bloom in colors bright,
Feeling fab under the sun's light.
Each petal serves a punchline fair,
A floral joke hangs in the air.

And when the wind brings news of fun,
The grasses sway, they've just begun.
With laughter bright, they share their cheer,
These veils of green hold secrets dear.

A Tapestry of Climbing Whispers

Vines weave tales in a tangled chat,
Each twist and turn, a friendly spat.
Climbing high to see what's near,
They roll their eyes while sipping cheer.

A curious snail stops for a peek,
At this lively, leafy boutique.
Sprouting buds wink and steal the show,
In this leafy circus, joy does grow.

The ivy jests under the moon,
Whispered secrets turn to a tune.
With frolicking ferns and joyous roots,
They entertain their leafy hoots.

So if you wander through the green,
And hear the laughter, bright and keen,
Just know it's nature's grand affair,
A tapestry woven with care.

The Soft Breath of the Green Grove

In a grove where giggles hide,
Trees share jokes on every side.
Mossy cushions hold their glee,
Making nature's comedy free.

The whispering winds say, 'Hey, listen!'
While dewdrops on leaves seem to glisten.
A rabbit pops out, gives a grin,
And hops around, let joy begin.

Flowers chuckle, swaying with ease,
In a gathering of buzzing bees.
Each gentle rustle tells a tale,
Of sunny banter, sweet and pale.

So come and sit in this fun-filled bower,
Where giggles bloom with each passing hour.
The green grove breathes with laughs so light,
In this realm of nature's sheer delight.

Climbing to the Heart of Nature

A squirrel invited me to climb,
He claimed the view was simply sublime.
I grabbed my snacks, a bottle of cheer,
Thought I'd find wisdom, but found a deer.

The trees giggled as I tripped on a root,
Birds started tweeting, "Hey, that's a hoot!"
I reached for a branch, feeling quite spry,
Only to realize it was an old guy.

He said, "Young lad, you ought to be wise,
Nature's got secrets, and mushrooms are spies."
I laughed so hard, I nearly fell down,
Who knew such wisdom lived in this town?

So here I am, with dirt on my face,
Chasing a rabbit, a whimsical race.
Nature is funny, a comic delight,
Each leaf tells a story beneath the sunlight.

The Poetry Beneath the Canopy

Under the branches, shadows so wide,
I found a frog who liked to confide.
He told me of stars and dreams in the mist,
While planning his world domination list.

A caterpillar wobbled, wearing a crown,
Declared himself ruler of this leafy town.
With a puffed-up chest, he gave quite the speech,
But couldn't quite find his balance to breach.

Nearby, a raccoon with manners quite posh,
Served acorns on dishes, a delicate nosh.
He said, "Join the feast, it's a nature affair,
We'll gossip 'bout humans who show up with flair."

With laughter and leftovers scattered around,
I felt poetry bloom without making a sound.
Under the canopy, life took its cue,
And the world felt much wittier, wouldn't you too?

Leaves of Untold Journeys

One leaf whispered tales of a daring flight,
Gone with the wind, in the pale moonlight.
It spoke of a sailor, lost in a breeze,
Who thought he could swim but just fell from trees.

A beetle marched proudly, with stripes of great pride,
Claimed he could conquer a mountain so wide.
Behind him a snail, with a shell home so grand,
Muttered, "At least I can carry my land!"

The sun shone bright, with a wink and a grin,
As bees buzzed by, joining in on the din.
"Let's dance," they all said, in wild jubilation,
Nature's a party, a grand celebration!

So off we all went on our whimsical quest,
With giggles, and snacks, feeling truly blessed.
Leaves of adventure, in laughter we roll,
Every corner a story, nature's own scroll.

Echoes Amongst Twisting Vines

In a garden where laughter thrives,
A snail gave a speech, oh what jive!
With twinkling eyes and a slimy charm,
He told of adventures, but meant no harm.

Around every corner, the vines would sway,
Eavesdropping secrets, come what may.
A wiggle-worm chuckled, wearing a tie,
As the sun rolled in with a mischievous eye.

The daisies danced, wearing their best,
While ants held a banquet, a tiny fest.
No shoes allowed on this enchanted ground,
Where giggles echoed, and joy was found.

So come join the fun, leave worries behind,
In a maze of green, where laughter's entwined.
For nature's oddities, we can't resist,
A splendid parade of the whimsical twist.

A Tangle of Shadows and Light

Underneath a leafy roof,
A squirrel played the fool, aloof.
He juggled acorns with such flair,
While butterflies giggled, without a care.

The shadows waltzed, as sunbeams stretched,
Through branches thick, their dance was etched.
A beetle declared, 'I'm the best chef here!'
Cooking up meals with a side of cheer.

Hiding behind a vine's embrace,
A chameleon joined, ready to race.
With colors so bright, he turned into cheese,
Leaving the garden buzzing with wheezes.

As night fell silent, the crickets played,
In this twisted tale, where mischief stayed.
A tangle of shadows, laughter so bold,
The wildest stories of nature retold.

Whispers in the Green Veil

Beneath a curtain of green so bright,
Frogs swapped tales of a moonlit night.
With croaks that echoed, they sang their song,
While fireflies danced, all night long.

A tiny gopher with a top hat proud,
Told his friends jokes, drawing a crowd.
He cracked up the bushes, made flowers sway,
In this leafy realm, where laughter played.

In a tangled thicket, whispers took flight,
As rabbits debated their favorite bite.
'Is it the carrot or the crunchy pea?'
Giggles burst forth like a wild jubilee.

So join in the fun, let the chatter rise,
In this vibrant world, spun with surprise.
For every vine tells secrets so sweet,
In a whimsical world, where critters meet.

Secrets Among the Vines

In a secret grove, two raccoons conspire,
To steal apples from trees, fuel their fire.
With sneaky moves and giggles galore,
They plotted and planned, but oh, the uproar!

A wise old owl, in a nest so cozy,
Spied on the duo, looking quite nosy.
He hooted with glee, 'What a clever pair!'
As the raccoons stumbled, unaware of their flair.

A hedgehog chimed in, rolling with glee,
'You'll never find apples, not with that spree!'
But the raccoons just laughed, and danced in the pines,
Crafting their mischief amid tangled vines.

As night drew close and shadows grew long,
They reveled in chaos, where they felt strong.
Among each vine, secrets did weave,
In this playful world, where tricksters believe.

A Garden of Secrets

In the garden where I hide,
The veggies gossip side by side.
Tomatoes flirt with thyme so sly,
While carrots challenge beet to fly.

A caterpillar joins the fun,
He wiggles like he's just begun.
The daisies laugh, they sway and bend,
Jokes about the bugs they send.

Gnomes with hats so crookedly worn,
Whisper secrets to the corn.
Now and then, the sun will beam,
On leafy laughter, like a dream.

So join this odd and silly place,
Where leafy friends embrace with grace.
Behind each stalk, a riddle waits,
In this garden full of mates.

The Realm of Shaded Conversations

Beneath the trees, the squirrels meet,
With acorns stacked, they form a seat.
They swap tall tales of daring feats,
While nibbling on their crunchy treats.

The owls hoot from their lofty perch,
Sharing gossip with a lonesome birch.
"I saw a cat that dared to creep,"
Said one, while others laughed and peeped.

In whispered tones, the shadows dance,
While leaves play tricks in a leafy trance.
Secrets linger in the breeze,
A world of jest beneath the trees.

So let the sun and moon conspire,
While creatures gather, never tire.
In this realm where laughter reigns,
Shaded conversations break the chains.

Hidden Journeys in the Canopy

High above where branches weave,
The creatures plot and misbelieve.
A raccoon rides a squirrel's back,
Singing songs of the forest track.

The leaves are plush with tales untold,
Of acorn heists and treasures bold.
"Who took my nut?" the squirrel cried,
As giggles echoed far and wide.

A parrot mocks the owl so wise,
"Your hoots are just a flat disguise!"
They share the sky, a vibrant sight,
In hidden journeys, pure delight.

So soar above, let laughter twine,
Through branches vast, where fun will shine.
In canopies, we find our cheer,
As nature's jest invites us near.

Blossoms in the Quiet Shadows

In the shadows where flowers peek,
They trade their funny little sneak.
Petals gossip, rustle low,
While bees buzz by, on their show.

A poppy whispers to a rose,
"Can you believe the gardener knows?"
With laughter thick as morning dew,
They murmur tales both fresh and new.

Late at night, the moon will wink,
As tulips plot and daisies think.
"Tomorrow's sun will bring us cheer,
More planted jokes will soon appear!"

So stroll through shadows, join the spree,
Where blossoms laugh, just like thee.
In quiet places, joy unfolds,
Within the shadows, stories told.

Serenity Among the Ivy Twists

In the garden where shadows play,
A squirrel juggles acorns all day,
The leaves whisper secrets with flair,
While frogs audition for a band up there.

Laughter dances on breezy trails,
As bees spin tunes with buzzing tales,
A ladybug twirls, breaks out in song,
While flowers join in—oh, what a throng!

Sunbeams peek through, casting a glow,
The snails race, but they're moving slow,
Critters gather for a giggling spree,
Amid the green, they're all wild and free.

So come join the fun beneath the leaves,
Where nature's humor is what it weaves,
In this playful patch of leafy cheer,
Laughter and joy are always near.

Veiled in Enchantment

A hedgehog dons a tiny hat,
As butterflies tease a playful cat,
The ivy smiles, all wrapped in green,
While pixies sit sipping tea, so serene.

A gnome tickles a sleepy toad,
As dandelions dance down the road,
With every rustle, a chuckle's born,
In this magical world, all worries are worn.

Each vine's a storyteller, tall and proud,
Whispering tales to the curious crowd,
The path ahead is a giggly quest,
Where even the shadows enjoy a jest.

So let's wander where the whimsy flows,
In enchanted realms where laughter grows,
Under the canopy, joy blooms alive,
In a world where the quirky simply thrive.

The Allure of Dappled Light

Sunlight winks through leafy beams,
While rabbits plot their daring dreams,
The shadows wiggle, inviting a peek,
As ants march in line, so orderly and sleek.

A chipmunk juggles berries, oh so grand,
While butterflies brush up the band,
They flit and flutter, a dazzling show,
In the dappled light, joy begins to glow.

Each vine a stage where the creatures play,
In the spotlight of sun, they laugh and sway,
The breeze carries giggles through the air,
A chatty parade without a care.

So roam through this space where merriment's bright,
In the charm of the day and the magic of night,
With every twist, the fun is just right,
In a world of laughter, bathed in light.

Budding Mysteries on Twining Stems

In the nooks where the mysteries grow,
A snail reads a book by the soft creek flow,
A hedgehog scribbles quirks on a leaf,
While crickets compose their comic relief.

Vines twist and turn like a playful dance,
As shadows leap in a quirky romance,
Mice put on shows with acorn hats,
While owls doze off in their cozy spats.

A remix of nature, with beats that inspire,
The flowers hum tunes with glee and desire,
Each petal's a note, creating great sound,
In this playful patch, joy's always found.

So let's embrace the whimsy we see,
Where laughter and wonders feel wild and free,
Among budding tales on twining stems,
Join in the fun, where delight never ends.

The Hidden Path of Growth

In a garden so wide, I found a sprout,
It waved to the sun, 'Hey, let's stand out!'
With worms doing yoga under the moss,
They whispered, 'Keep growing, no need to gloss!'

A snail held a meeting, with ants in the lead,
They shared their own tales, as sprouts take heed.
'Life's no sprint,' they laughed, 'it's a slow crawl,
But hey, that's a plan, let's dance through it all!'

Tadpoles in suits talked stock market trends,
While butterflies argued on fashion, their bends.
The daisies shook petals in giggly delight,
As blooms popped their heads, just to join the flight!

So here's to the sprouts, and paths yet untold,
With humor in growth, let our stories unfold.
When life starts to tangle, just take a big leap,
And let laughter, not worries, be what you keep!

The Green Sanctuary Awaits

In the midst of the leaves, I saw a grand throne,
A squirrel in shades claimed it all as his own.
'With acorns for snacks and a crown made of grass,
This forest life rocks! Why let moments pass?'

The ferns held a party, all dressed up in shade,
They boogied with beetles, a wild serenade.
'We'll dance through the night, to the tunes of the breeze,
While mossy rocks chuckle, they're as old as the trees!'

Parrots chimed in, 'Let's talk of the day,
How the sun throws a rave, brightening our play!'
With shadows for partners, they spun round and round,
In a whimsical whirl, joy joyously found.

So dance with the leaves in this sanctuary green,
Embrace all the quirks that the wild can convene.
For in every small giggle, a grand tale would sow,
And happiness thrives where the wild breezes flow!

Whispers of the Wild Climb

Up high in the branches, where giggles take flight,
A raccoon had charcoal for art, pure delight.
With branches for stages and squirrels on the mic,
They crooned all their favorites, oh what a hike!

The bees formed a band, buzzing sweet little tunes,
While spiders spun webs like glittering moons.
The laughter echoed, as they twirled with the breeze,
Celebrating the chaos, a party with ease!

A chameleon whispered, 'I blend in with flair,
But I'm really a riot with colors to share!'
And the owls hooted wisdom, just under their breath,
'In this climb of our lives, we'll find joy, not death!'

So rise through the branches, chase laughter's embrace,
In a wild climb of fun, there's a special place.
Where creatures and critters weave joy with a wink,
And life's not a worry, but a whimsical link!

In the Embrace of the Twined Roots

Beneath the old oak, roots tangled like dreams,
A party of gophers formed long-lasting teams.
With veggies on sticks and a root beer parade,
They danced to the rhythms, all worries delayed.

The rabbits were racing with ribbons galore,
While the hedgehogs brought snacks, who could ask for more?
With flora and fauna, they crafted a show,
Holding hands in the earth, their spirits would grow!

In the shade of the trunk, bright laughter would ring,
As fireflies painted the night with a sting.
'Life's just a picnic,' a critter would chirp,
With humor and friendship, we all are a blurp!

So bond with the roots in this magical tune,
Where laughter and joy are forever in bloom.
In every small nook, let the fun take its flight,
Bound by twining stories that sparkle so bright!

Under the Green Archway

Beneath the leaves, a squirrel pranced,
With acorns dancing, he took a chance.
A bird in tow, chirping in rhyme,
Counting its eggs, oh, what a crime!

A garden gnome, with a cheeky grin,
Wants to join in, but can't quite fit in.
The roses chuckle, petals so bright,
As they plot to prank him late at night.

A playful breeze brings whispers near,
While tags on vines spell out 'Do not fear!'
Laughter echoes through the verdescent wood,
Where even the mushrooms wish they could.

Oh, the tales they weave, threaded with glee,
In secret corners, where none can see.
With every step, there's mischief afoot,
As the green archway sways in the soot.

A Dance Among the Twists

In the maze of hues, oh what a sight,
A tortoise twirls in the low moonlight.
With hedges as partners, they swirl and sway,
As insects applaud at the end of the day.

A wily fox plays the fiddle with flair,
While bunnies jump high without any care.
The daisies wave, trying to keep pace,
While others just giggle, lost in their space.

Round and round in a leafy embrace,
Laughter erupts, a wild, joyous race.
The path's a conundrum, yet never in vain,
For friendship blooms in the twisty domain.

The stars peek through, the night tastes of fun,
And all gather round, each one and everyone.
In their dance, no worries make a trace,
Just a party beneath a green lace.

The Secret Keepers of the Attic

Up in the loft, old treasures lie,
With dust bunnies leaping and dreaming high.
A bear with sunglasses guards the stash,
While an old clock giggles, tick-tock and splash!

The boxes are stacked, tales unfold,
Where memories sing and laughter is gold.
A former knight in armor now rusts,
But joins in the chatter, sparking our trust.

An owl with spectacles charts the map,
Of all hidden paths, where secrets unwrap.
What's that over there? A hat with three sides,
Saves jokes for the brave and the merry who bide.

So gather round, friends, let's hear the lore,
Of mischief and giggles, and maybe a snore.
In the corners of time, where treasures lay,
The attic's a circus, where fun leads the way.

Enigmas Wrapped in Greenery

Hiding in vines, a riddle takes flight,
A frog wearing glasses, a curious sight.
He croaks out a joke, oh what a tease,
Revealing the punchline among the leaves.

The ivy giggles, tangling the truth,
As squirrels inquire about the wise sleuth.
"I'm here for the chase," said the sly little sprite,
"Why dance with the shadows when you can delight?"

A bushy-tailed friend shares puns with a grin,
While the flowers debate if they should jump in.
The wind carries whispers, oh what a scheme,
To unravel the verses, it feels like a dream.

In each twist and turn lives a laughter-filled tale,
Of bumbles and blunders, of playful detail.
So wander on through the greenery vast,
Where enigmas unfold, and joy's unsurpassed.

Where the Mossed Paths Lead

In tangled greens where squirrels play,
The paths of moss will lead the way.
A frog's a knight in emerald sheen,
He croaks, 'Welcome to my leafy scene!'

A hedgehog twirls, he thinks he's spry,
While ants march on in neat, brief sighs.
What secrets hide in shadows thick?
Perhaps a gnome with painted stick!

The breeze is giggling through the leaves,
A whisper of mischief that deceives.
Oh, what a show of nature's jest,
Where every creature strives to impress!

So grab your boots, let's hop and twine,
In this green maze, let's sip on wine!
With nature's laughs and stories told,
We'll dance with joy, both brave and bold.

Threads of Time in the Lush Depths

In whispers now the past slips by,
While vines weave tales, oh my, oh my!
A rabbit sneezes – what a giggle!
And bee-boys buzz with cha-cha wiggle!

A lizard dives, a comical flip,
Leaves flutter down like they've lost their grip.
Each thread of green holds laughs galore,
From shadowed glades to the forest floor!

A squirrel juggles acorns with flair,
While daisies gossip without a care.
And moss, so plush, wears a grin so wide,
Inviting all to join the ride!

What joy it is to roam these trails,
Where even the wind sings silly tales.
So let's embrace the giggly rhyme,
In nature's arms, we'll bide our time!

The Enigma in the Greenery

Beneath the leaves, a riddle stirs,
A chicken walks, dressed in furs!
The fawn debates with a wise old owl,
While mushrooms giggle, 'Oh, what a prowl!'

In vines that twist, do secrets lie?
Do raccoons plot? Oh my, oh my!
The gnarled roots twirl like ballet feet,
While shadows dance to a jazzy beat!

A bear spins tales of his picnic fright,
As fireflies blink in the velvet night.
And who knew loons could tell a joke?
As laughter reigns beneath the oak!

Let's frolic here where whimsy reigns,
In leafy lanes with playful chains.
Come leap and bound in this merry spree,
In a world of green, come join the tea!

Labyrinth of Nature's Embrace

Through tendrils green, we weave a thread,
Where even the lost find cheer instead.
A turtle's hat spins round and round,
While butterflies chuckle, lost and found!

The elder tree bows low with charm,
It says, 'Fear not! You'll come to no harm.'
A muddy pig, with style so grand,
Slips on leaves and tumbles, oh what a stand!

Mossy paths with giggles sing,
While lambs prance dressed in their spring fling.
A maze of mirth awaits ahead,
With hidden puns in flowers spread!

So take a stroll, let laughter flow,
In nature's hold, we're all aglow.
For in this maze, the heart finds grace,
With humor stitched in every space!

In the Heart of the Twisted Realm

In a garden of green, where the odd things grow,
Laughter twists with roots, putting on quite the show.
Rabbits wear hats, and the daisies giggle,
Playing hopscotch with shadows, they dance and wiggle.

The squirrels throw nuts, hoping to score,
While the owls hoot tunes, wanting an encore.
Frogs serenade crickets under the moon,
Their croaks harmonize, an unlikely tune.

Gnomes in a circle, they spin and they whirl,
Juggling tomatoes, what a strange world!
Forget your troubles; come join in the fun,
In this realm of oddities, laughter's never done.

Pathway to Serendipity

Stumbling through thickets, I trip on a vine,
Find a treasure map drawn by a raccoon so fine.
Each footstep uncovers a laugh and a cheer,
As dandelions whisper, 'Oh dear, oh dear!'

Butterflies flutter, wearing polka dot suits,
Jumping through puddles in laughter-filled boots.
With every wrong turn, there's a joke to behold,
Every twist of the path, a story retold.

The mushrooms are chatting, they seem quite aware,
Of the silly dance moves in warm autumn air.
As I giggle and stumble, just trying to see,
This pathway of joy leads right back to me.

Whispers of Enchanted Growth

Underneath leafy boughs, secrets are spun,
With vines making jokes, oh what puzzling fun!
A wilted old flower, with humor, imparts,
"Don't fret, dear young bud, bloom straight from your heart!"

The mushrooms giggle, they pop up and tease,
While tangled-up roots whisper jokes on the breeze.
Each vine a comedian, rooting for glee,
Entwined in the joy, they're as happy as can be.

I tiptoe on petals, avoiding the bees,
As blossoms form laughter, carried by the breeze.
Nature's sweet comedy, never too shy,
With every new sprout, it's the perfect reply.

Beneath the Canopy of Time

Beneath ancient branches, I find joy galore,
Leaves laughing softly, who could ask for more?
With each tick of the clock, the trees share a joke,
Telling tales of the past, as the old branches croak.

Dancing with shadows, the sun starts to tease,
In this merry forest, they sway with the breeze.
A wise old oak chuckles and shares with a grin,
"Life's all about laughter; let the fun begin!"

Lost in this moment, I swing with delight,
As the stars wink above in the blanket of night.
With whimsy inside, I cherish each rhyme,
For here, under laughter, exists a grand time.

Entwined in Nature's Secrets

Beneath the leaves, a squirrel plots,
With acorns stashed, he ties some knots.
A dance of shadows, sneaky peek,
He snickers low, 'It's mine to keep!'

The vines are thick, they wrap around,
With every twist, new jokes abound.
A rabbit snorts, a garden prank,
He hops away, no time to tank.

The flowers giggle, petals high,
While butterflies play on clouds of sky.
They swirl about, in hues so bright,
Each chuckle echoes, pure delight.

And while we laugh, let's weave our tales,
In tangled greens where humor sails.
The world is nuts, let joy be found,
In nature's arms, we'll twirl around.

Between the Twists of Time

A turtle chuckles, slow but sly,
He blinks and grins, 'Just watch me fly.'
With every twist a story flows,
Of mossy paths and muddy toes.

The whispers gather, roots intertwine,
They gossip low, 'Who looks so fine?'
A hedgehog winks, his quills so sharp,
"The hedges sing, just hear them harp."

The clock ticks softly, branches sway,
A bumblebee steals time away.
He buzzes loud, with candy sweet,
"Who's got the time for empty feet?"

And as we stroll through leafy lanes,
With laughter echoing, joy remains.
Between the twists, let's all unwind,
In every leaf, new fun we find.

Stories in the Greenery

In tangled roots, a tale unfolds,
Of daring deeds and secrets told.
A ladybug with tiny specs,
She giggles loud, "I'm due some checks!"

The spider spins his threads so fine,
A web of jokes, an art divine.
He catches flies and snickers sweet,
"Life's a trap, can't take a seat!"

The ferns sway gently, secrets shared,
Each rustle tells of fun declared.
A chameleon grins, blending in,
"Where's my snack? My big win-win!"

And as we wander through the green,
With playful pranks, we'll laugh unseen.
The stories tell, the laughter flows,
In every twist, our joy just grows.

Veins of the Silent Grove

In silent groves, the whispers dwell,
A babbling brook, it thinks it's swell.
With stones that laugh, in splashes bright,
They might just start a splashy fight!

The owls hoot tales, wise yet sly,
With rolling eyes, they watch us try.
A fox struts past, in cheeky flair,
"Don't trip on roots, or lose your hair!"

The sunbeams dance on leaves like gold,
They wink and nudge, their warmth so bold.
A chipmunk laughs, "I've lost the race,
But stole the snack — it made my face!"

In nature's arms, let's spin around,
With all the laughter, joy is found.
In veins of green, our hearts will play,
A grand ballet, come join the sway!

The Tangle of Forgotten Dreams

In a garden where socks just roam,
Tangled twirls in their leafy home.
Gnomes chuckle at the socks they find,
Laughing loudly, all intertwined.

A cat plays tag with the ivy green,
Pouncing softly, a fluffy machine.
Forgetful whispers weave through the air,
Dreams are lost in the playful affair.

Socks dance freely, twirling round,
Chasing shadows from the ground.
Hats and pails join in the fray,
In this garden, they come to play.

Once was a hat, now just a ghost,
Jokes on the breeze, the ivy's host.
Amidst the laughter, dreams drift away,
Yet socks keep dancing, come what may.

Beneath the Tendrils' Grasp

The tendrils tickle, a gentle tease,
While squirrels play hide and seek with ease.
Underneath the leafy dome they frolic,
A comedy show, quite symbolic.

Toads in tuxedos leap with flair,
Waving hello to the frogs that stare.
Mice in top hats twirl in delight,
A tea party happening, oh, what a sight!

Beneath the rich green, secrets unfold,
Whispers of laughter, tales to be told.
In this viney maze, the wild convenes,
Crafting new laws of silly routines.

As sunlight glimmers on the scene,
With every tumble, they squeak and preen.
In the grasp of the curls and sways,
Life's a joke in whimsical ways.

Lurking in the Lushness

In shadows thick, a creature peeks,
With googly eyes, it squirms and sneaks.
A porcupine planning a prank for fun,
Hiding amidst the leaves, just one.

Vines like lollipops, twist and twine,
Caterpillars giggle, sipping on brine.
The ferns shake hands with roots and bugs,
Throwing a party for all the chugs.

Late-night meetings in the damp, green light,
Talking about dreams that take flight.
All the critters uniting with glee,
Plotting marathons, a wild jamboree!

In the lushness where frolic reigns,
Sunlit afternoons and starry lanes.
Amidst the laughter and playful tease,
Life tiptoes joyfully, dancing with ease.

Echoes of Verdant Thought

Leaves whisper secrets, the trees confide,
In a merry dance, they let joy slide.
A parrot laughs, perched high in the air,
Mocking the funny tales that they share.

The vines murmur tunes of olden days,
Echoing chuckles in twisted ways.
Frogs keep croaking their rhythmic rhymes,
While ants march along in silly lines.

In every nook and cranny alive,
A carnival of thoughts, they connive.
With a gust of wind, the laughter grows,
As even the mushrooms wear silly bows.

And so the garden, vibrant and bright,
Echoes with laughter, a pure delight.
In verdant thoughts, all worries levitate,
Embracing the joy, let's celebrate!

A Journey Through the Wild Embrace

In tangled greens, we leap and roll,
A squirrel mocks our clumsy stroll.
Chasing shadows, we lose the map,
While sunbeams giggle, 'Hey! Take a nap!'

With vines that dance and tickle our nose,
We find our way through the leafy prose.
A rabbit hops by, gives us a wink,
And suddenly ponder, do plants even think?

The more we laugh, the more we fall,
As bushes whisper, 'Come have a ball!'
With sticky hands and berry-stained cheeks,
We join the wild as it playfully squeaks.

A journey it seems, yet we're still the same,
Two garden gnomes, lost in a game.
Through laughter and folly, we make our mark,
In this wild embrace, we've got quite the spark.

Where the Ferns Gently Swell

A forest teems with jokes untold,
Each fern a wink, each leaf a fold.
We dance in circles, arms in the air,
As critters giggle without a care.

A raccoon shimmies, wearing our hats,
While deer roll their eyes at our silly spats.
The ferns chuckle, they swish and sway,
"Welcome to our party, come out and play!"

With every step, we trip and slide,
The wild's our stage, we take it in stride.
From flowers to fungus, it's quite the jest,
In this frolicsome realm, we are at our best.

So we'll laugh with the ferns and frolic around,
In this dizzying maze of the playful ground.
As dusk settles in, we'll gather and cheer,
In the laughter of leaves, there's nothing to fear.

Caressing the Secrets of the Past

With vines that curl like whispers of old,
We stumble upon tales that never grow cold.
A gnarled old tree holds secrets so bold,
While squirrels conspire, the laughter unfolds.

Each leaf is a page, each branch a line,
As we recount stories over a glass of brine.
The ghosts of the garden invite us to play,
While the sun keeps shining in glorious array.

"Remember that time?" we giggle and snort,
As shadows dance in a hilarious court.
The past comes alive with each silly quip,
And nature's secrets begin to skip.

So let's caress the memories dear,
In this wild, whimsical atmosphere.
With friends by our side, we'll spin tall tales,
As laughter echoes and friendship prevails.

The Berry Of Forgotten Days

In hidden corners of sweet summer's hue,
Lie berries that giggle, calling me and you.
With each berry pluck, a memory pops,
As laughter erupts, and the fun never stops.

A blue one says, "Hey, remember that time?"
When we painted our faces, oh what a crime!
The red ones chime in, "Don't let it go!"
"Come share in our laughter, we'll steal the show!"

With juice on our fingers, and smiles so bright,
We feast on the past, from morning till night.
Each berry a fountain of sweet, funny lore,
In this riotous garden, we long to explore.

So come, pluck a berry, take a big bite,
And let the laughter carry through the night.
When forgotten days blossom, it's truly a blast,
In this fruity escapade, let's make memories last.

The Climbing Mysteries

In my quest for the top of the fence,
I stumbled on roots that make no sense.
They giggled and wiggled, a mischievous bunch,
While I teetered and tottered, not sure to lunch.

A squirrel named Fred had the best view,
He pointed and laughed as I fell in the dew.
"You're climbing all wrong!" he chattered with glee,
As I wrestled with branches, stuck like a bee.

The leaves cheered me on, so cheerful and bright,
Encouraging laughter as I took flight.
I swore they conspired to keep me at bay,
While they whispered their secrets and danced the day away.

At last, I ascended with leaves in my hair,
Only to find that the air was too rare.
The mysteries lingered, serenely they glowed,
As I pondered the climb—as I hiccupped and flowed.

Serenity Beneath Woven Leaves

Under the canopy, life takes a pause,
Where mischief is woven with whimsical laws.
The sun peeks through gaps like a prankster in bloom,
Casting shadows that dance in the whimsical room.

A raccoon named Lilly had a secret to tell,
Of pastries and picnics, she rang the lunch bell.
"Bring your own snack, and don't mind the ants,
They'll steal your jelly if given the chance!"

Under the leaves, the banter was grand,
With squirrels doing cartwheels—oh, weren't they so planned?
It's a feast of odd tales; a carnival cheer,
In this woven domain, no room for a fear.

A chorus of chuckles, they pull at my sleeve,
"Join our shenanigans; who wants to leave?"
In tranquility's arms, I snicker and sway,
As the canopy giggles, guiding my way.

The Silhouettes Beneath the Ivy

Shadows are dancing in mid-afternoon,
Dressed in costumes from leaves, a funny cartoon.
The branches are whispering secrets so sly,
As I twist and I turn, fulfilling their lie.

A fox suddenly pranced with a grin on his face,
He claimed to have mastered the art of the chase.
"With that leap you just made, I demand a show,
Or I'll bring out my hat and steal to the low!"

Crickets strummed music, uncoordinated, loud,
While peas in the pod formed a comedic crowd.
The turtles, they bobbed in a frivolous spin,
In shadows that jiggle, where laughter begins.

Sunshine and giggles create a wild mix,
As I sway with the sillies, feeling the tricks.
In silhouettes trailing, my spirit takes flight,
Beneath all the laughter, everything feels right.

Embrace of the Untold Stories

Every vine holds a tale, with humor and zest,
From the sycamore's laughter to the elm's jest.
A caterpillar's wiggle, a bug's clumsy dance,
In the embrace of the leaves, they twirl and prance.

A gnome with a shovel was digging for gold,
"I lost my last treasure, or so I was told!"
But when I peeked closer, he chuckled aloud,
"It's gone for good! I weep, but am proud!"

Under this quilt of green mystery spun,
The world seems so silly when life's meant for fun.
A frog wearing glasses recites poems in rhyme,
While the roses all giggle at his old-timer mime.

With each little whisper, an uproar unfolds,
Each laugh and each tale, another joy holds.
In the stories of leaves, conspiracies play,
As I nestle within, making jokes of the day.

The Enchanted Grove's Memoir

In a grove where squirrels play,
A wise old owl holds sway.
With acorns stacked up high,
He claims to reach the sky.

The trees wear hats of green,
While dancing leaves are seen.
A party brewed in shade,
Where giggles never fade.

A rabbit sports a bowtie,
While crickets dance nearby.
A snicker from the brook,
As tricky roots, they took.

In this quirky little space,
Nature wears a funny face.
With every twist and turn,
A new tale you will learn.

Converging Paths in Nature's Silk

Two paths wove side by side,
One led to a fly's wild ride.
Another whispered soft and sweet,
Where ladybugs and beetles meet.

The grass held secrets, worn and wise,
With ants in suits, they chart the skies.
A three-legged frog was quite the guide,
Remarked, 'It's fun on this wild slide!'

A trail of petals led the way,
Inviting all to come and play.
While shadows danced on woven streams,
Nature giggles amidst daydreams.

With each step taken on this ground,
The funny moments know no bound.
Nature's charm in every nook,
Is a page right from a storybook.

Climbing Dreams of the Verdant Realm

In a forest thick with cheer,
Laughter echoes far and near.
A tree with branches like arms wide,
Says, 'Come climb, don't you hide!'

The raccoon's on a skateboard ride,
Flipping over roots with pride.
A flower giggles in the breeze,
Telling jokes to bumblebees.

A squirrel dons a tiny crown,
Declaring himself the king of town.
His subjects, fungi, bow and curtsy,
While worms just wiggle in a flurry.

Each leaf a canvas of sly fun,
Nature's jest has just begun.
In this realm where giggles blend,
Every twist brings joy 'til end.

Nature's Hidden Tapestry

Beneath a canopy of laughs,
Playful vines hide snickers' paths.
A hedgehog in a tutu spun,
Declared, 'Oh look, it's time for fun!'

The flowers wear their brightest hues,
While mushrooms share their latest news.
A cricket's serenade rings clear,
To every creature gathered near.

A treasure map of leaves unfurls,
With riddles told by swaying swirls.
The breeze makes funny faces too,
As petals waft like bright balloons.

In this realm, hilarity reigns,
Where sunshine dances, joy remains.
Take a step, you'll find it near,
A hidden laugh, a world sincere.

The Hidden Pathways of Green

In a forest where squirrels run and hide,
There's a path less traveled, oh what a ride.
With branches that wiggle, and vines that dance,
You might trip over roots if you give it a chance.

The flowers gossip in colors so bright,
They giggle and whisper from morning to night.
A snail on the road claims he's the fastest,
While a turtle rolls by, slow but the craftiest.

You'd think you'd get lost in these tangled vines,
But the frogs will guide you, singing their lines.
Their croaks and their ribbits give quite the show,
As they hop to the rhythm, all ready to go.

So, grab your old boots and don't mind the mess,
In this jolly green jungle, it's all about jest.
With a twist and a turn, you'll find such a scene,
In the hidden pathways of glorious green.

Enchantment in the Overgrowth

In the underbrush rich with laughter and cheer,
The lizards wear sunglasses, the sun's shining clear.
With butterflies flitting, all dressed for a ball,
While ants play a game of bug hide-and-seek call.

The mushrooms are holding a curious feast,
With toadstools as tables—it's quite the beast!
The caterpillars groove, their moves so divine,
They'll show you their skills, just wait for the sign.

The vines bend and stretch, they twirl to the beat,
While bees buzz along, bringing nectar so sweet.
The hedgehogs roll in, their eyes wide with glee,
Dancing through thickets, as happy as can be.

So if you need laughter, just wander this way,
Let nature's delight be a game that you play.
In the overgrown charm, there's magic for all,
And the antics of nature will surely enthrall.

Fragments of Nature's Enigma

Among the tall grasses where whispers abound,
A riddle unfolds in the sights all around.
The dandelions chuckle, their seeds take to flight,
As the busy bees bumble, making things right.

The twigs have opinions, they snap in dismay,
At the thumping of feet on this wild, wacky way.
The mushrooms are winking, a trickster's delight,
While the sun peeks through leaves, a warm golden light.

The squirrels bring news of a secret debate,
Who's faster in life, the hedgehog or mate?
While frogs claim their kingdom from under the logs,
And declare with a croak, they'll duel with the dogs.

In this puzzle of trees, the answers may hide,
So dive into chaos, let nonsense be your guide.
For nature's enigma is wrapped up in fun,
And each quirky moment shines just like the sun.

Beneath the Leafy Labyrinth

In the leafy maze where the shadows play tricks,
The branches all whisper their cleverest picks.
With an owl in the corner, plotting his next meal,
And a mouse on the run, spinning quite the wheel.

The hedges are buzzing with gossip galore,
As the flowers swap stories, they never bore.
The rabbits, they tangle in a dance, oh so spry,
While the wind carries tales to the clouds up on high.

The wild berries chuckle, a feast on the way,
Pleasantly tart as they tempt and they sway.
You'll trip on a root, but don't take it to heart,
For each little stumble is just nature's art.

So wander this tangle with a grin and a laugh,
For hidden delights hide beyond every path.
In the leafy labyrinth, where the funny things play,
You'll find joy in the madness, come join the ballet!

Lush Embrace of the Forgotten

In the shadows where whispers play,
A frog holds court at the end of the day.
He croaks his tales, a royal decree,
While fireflies dance, all wild and free.

Mossy carpets beneath my toes,
Tickle my feet, it's how laughter grows.
The squirrels plot mischief, so sly and spry,
As they steal my sandwich; oh how they fly!

Beneath the blooms, a picnic awaits,
But ants conspire, stealthy as mates.
They swarm like ninjas, so bold and spry,
I'm left alone, with only a sigh.

In this wild realm, where giggles unfold,
Each bramble a joke, a tale to be told.
Embracing the chaos, with every fling,
Nature's embrace is a comical thing.

Cradled by Nature's Threads

A spider spins stories in shimmering strands,
While I take a break, in the soft, mossy lands.
A snore from a badger, a hiccup from me,
While daisies lean close, as if they could see.

The trees share their secrets in rustling sighs,
I giggle along as a bird fluffs and flies.
The sun winks down like a mischievous friend,
Oh, how I ponder what tricks it may send.

With sun hats made out of fern and of grass,
The critters all gather to gossip and pass.
A squirrel called Agnes announces a feast,
Two nuts and a berry – she says it's a treat!

Where shadows and laughter weave in a dance,
Each twig is a punchline, each leaf is a chance.
Cradled in threads of the wild's vibrant bloom,
Life is a giggle, not just a costume.

The Buried Truth of the Ferns

Under the ferns, there's treasure untold,
A world where the shy become brave and bold.
The worms share their wisdom on soil's delight,
While I look for gold, but just find a bite.

The roots tell of mischief beneath the cool shade,
Where will-o'-the-wisps throw a glittering parade.
The mushrooms engage in an annual race,
But I trip on a rock; oh, what an embrace!

Toadstools and dandelions conspire and laugh,
Plotting adventures, yet doing the math.
"Who can tiptoe past the slumbering bugs?"
They cheer for the one who triumphs with shrugs.

The buried truth is a rollicking jest,
Among leafy whispers, they host quite a fest.
In nature's own sitcom, with each twist, each turn,
There's comedy waiting; for that, I do yearn.

In the Heart of the Leafy Hideaway

In a leafy nook where the giggles reside,
A family of rabbits all dance in their stride.
They hop and they tumble, their noses a-twitch,
While singing of carrots, oh what a rich pitch!

A turtle named Ted takes the path, very slow,
While pondering life in the soft, green glow.
He laughs at the hares, "Oh, what a delight!
You scurry and whirl, but I'll win this night!"

Among tangled vines, a raccoon drops down,
With snacks in his paws and a sly, silly frown.
"Who wants to share this baked berry pie?"
But it's gone in a flash; oh, how time does fly!

The trees lean in closely to hear all the fun,
While squirrels juggle acorns, one, two, then done.
In this leafy hideaway, laughter's the way,
As we frolic in flora, come dance, come play.

Embracing the Hidden Canopy

In the garden, leaves collide,
Squirrels dance with leafy pride.
The branches swing, what a sight,
As birds wear hats, oh what a fright!

A hidden world beneath the green,
Where laughter echoes, light and keen.
Mice on swings, oh what a show,
The trees just giggle, 'Come and go!'

Hats made of twigs and sticks they wear,
Rabbits hop without a care.
In this space, we spin around,
For joy is found beneath the crown!

So here we bounce and laugh with glee,
In nature's club, just you and me.
Embracing all that hides in view,
Our silly fun is never through!

Shadows of the Climbing Leaves

The shadows whisper silly tunes,
As dandelions dance with the moons.
A caterpillar bugs a bee,
'Let's race!' it shouts, and off they flee.

Lizards play leapfrog on a nook,
While crickets gather round to look.
A game of tag beneath the vines,
Where everyone giggles, life aligns.

Leaves tickle noses, all around,
Grasshoppers leap, they're joy unbound.
With nature's orchestra in the air,
Life's a laugh, without a care!

So join the fun under the trees,
Where shadows mingle with the breeze.
In leafy realms of pure delight,
We play and joke, from morn till night!

Treading the Twisted Path

Here I stroll on winding trails,
Through tangled vines and funny tales.
A goat in boots prances with cheer,
While dancing logs jump with a sneer!

Bump into a hedgehog, oh dear!
It mutters, 'What's all this ruckus here?'
A twist and turn, and suddenly,
The foliage giggles, 'Join the spree!'

Marshmallow clouds pop in the sky,
And flower hats ask the bees to fly.
With every step, a new surprise,
As laughter twinkles in our eyes.

So along the path, we skip and hop,
In nature's realm, we'll never stop.
Life's a jest, on this journey wide,
With every leaf, a friend beside!

Beneath the Verdant Cloak

Under leafy canopies, we hide,
Where whispers curl and giggles ride.
A raccoon chef brews acorn stew,
While owls critique the forest view.

Beneath this cloak of vibrant green,
Nature throws a zany scene.
With ferns in hats, they march with pride,
Joking trees stand side by side.

The mushrooms play a peculiar tune,
As snails go sliding, oh how they swoon!
With every twist, a joyful jest,
In every root lies a hidden quest.

So come and laugh amongst the leaves,
In this secret realm where fun retrieves.
Beneath the cloak where spirits soar,
The tales are rich, forevermore!

www.ingramcontent.com/pod-product-compliance
Lightning Source LLC
Chambersburg PA
CBHW071841160426
43209CB00003B/377